WHEW WE...I'M FREE!
When Life Tries to Break You

LaVonne Gravely Sanders

Dedication

This book is dedicated to my deceased Mother, Brenda Moss. I miss you terribly and I wish you were still here with me. I know that you're watching over me and I hope that I've made you proud. I love you Mom.

Acknowledgements

First giving honor to God, the head of my life.
Charnika Elliott, thank you so much for your wisdom,
prayers and encouragement. To my family and
friends, thank you for your constant support, I
couldn't have done this without you.

TABLE OF CONTENT

To assist you with this book after every chapter there will be a set of discussion questions for your personal reflection or book club.

INTRODUCTION

Growing up I remember dreaming of being a high fashion model. I wanted to grace the cover of magazines and walk the red carpet at the largest Hollywood events. I also wanted to marry the man of my dreams. He would be tall, handsome and he would ride in on a white horse and sweep me off my feet. Now as an adult, who knew that life would be filled with so many challenges and tough decisions.

Not having a father present in my life shaped the woman the I became. It's unfortunate, but I know a lot of the choices I've made was due to not having my father present consistently. Little girls should be the apple of their father's eye. He should be the first man that we fall in love with. The first man that we learn to trust and the first man to have our backs. That wasn't the case for me, so I looked everywhere else for this type of love.

I've learned that with every choice there are consequences and I've also learned that what goes around comes around. Karma is not friendly and she doesn't discriminate. One minute you're on cloud nine and the next minute, life comes tumbling down on you like a ton of bricks. If you're not strong enough to endure the blows life will quickly take you to deep dark place called depression.

I have a private love affair with depression, she tries to consume me on a regular basis and if I'm not careful she wins quite often. Strength, resiliency and endurance are things that I try to maintain to stay out of that dark hole. It's not always easy and I fall often. The key is to dust yourself off and keep trying. My favorite quote and scripture, Peter 5:10 -The suffering won't last forever. It won't be long before this genius God who has great plans for us in Christ.

CHAPTER ONE

DID I DO THAT

I can't believe it's 1989, I'm running around in life day to day without any plans for my life, no ambition, no drive. I only work part time and the rest of the time I'm hanging out late with my friends. One day I woke up and decided that a change was needed and needed immediately. I decided that I would go take the test to join the military. "Why not," is what I said to myself?" I would be able to travel the world for free and I wouldn't have very many bills to pay. A few weeks passed and it was time for me to take the test, I was extremely nervous and unsure of my decision. I passed the test, my goal was to join the Air Force but my score wasn't high enough so I accepted an offer to join the U.S. Army.

Within a few short months, I was packed and ready to report for duty. There was a ceremony conducted where all new inductees had to be sworn in. We stood in front of high ranking military officials and several flags, there was also a red carpet. In that moment, with my right hand up and my left hand on my chest, I began to have my very first ever panic attack. I didn't know what was happening other than my heart was racing very fast and I was extremely nervous. It felt like I was having a heart attack and I was scared to death. OH MY GOD, what have I done!

I started basic training in Fort Jackson, S.C., and life suddenly became very different for me. I was being told what to do, when to do it, and how to do it and I didn't like it. When you sign your life over to Uncle Sam, you're his property for at least 8 years. There were hundreds of new soldiers going through basic training, which consisted of a bunch of tests and preparations for your specific job responsibilities. We were assigned bunk mates or a buddy as they called it. You were responsible for that person and she was responsible for you. My bunk mate was a Puerto Rican girl named Sandy and boy was she a firecracker. She tended not to follow any of the rules which kept us both in a lot of trouble. I started meeting a lot of great people and things didn't seem to be turning out to bad. I successfully graduated from basic training and then moved on to school to learn my trade.

Sandy and I attended the same school, we had the same job assignments. I was glad to still have her by my side. We became very close friends and began to really depend on each other. One night Sandy and I decided to sneak out to go to a party. We knew that we were breaking the rule, new soldiers were not allowed to hang out with active duty personnel. When we arrived at the venue there were some military officers at the door checking identifications. One of the officers was a very handsome looking man who immediately caught my eye and I caught his. He followed me inside and we began to talk and we immediately fell for each other. We started dating and things began to move very quickly. Within those few weeks, he asked me to marry him! I was so infatuated with him and didn't hesitate to say "YES!" We went to the courthouse and made it official, I was now a married woman!

Shortly after the marriage, my husband got orders to relocate to another base in VA, about an hour away. I wasn't happy about the move but we would be able to see each other on the weekends. I decided to pack up and pay my husband a visit one weekend. It was surprise and he didn't know that I was coming. When I walked in to surprise him, I was the one surprised because there he laid with a woman in the bed with him. I didn't know whether to scream or run, I ran. I didn't say a word and in that moment I knew I had made the biggest mistake of my life marrying this man. I couldn't believe what happened and I was deeply hurt and numb. A week later, I filed for an annulment.

Chapter One Discussion

What are some things that stood out to you in this chapter?

Would you have handled things differently, if so how?

What lessons did you learn if any?

CHAPTER TWO

BYE BYE BABY!

I can't believe I was able to get out of the military due to pregnancy. I'm not sure how I feel at the moment because I'm carrying a child by my husband, whom I caught in the bed with another woman. I must say that I'm glad to be back home with my Mom. Of course, she's not happy with me because having children is the last thing that she wanted for me, especially at this age. My Mom is and has always been very opinionated about my decisions. Let's see how this pregnancy goes.

It's now a month after discharging from the U.S Army and I'm slowly readjusting to civilian life again. I woke up early to start looking for a job so that I'll be able to move out on my own when the baby is born. Living with my Mom and Stepfather is not an option. Getting away from home is one of the reasons I joined the military anyway.

I got in the shower to start my day. I started having really bad cramps and the next thing I know I looked down and blood was pouring out of me in every direction. I grabbed a towel and screamed for my Mom to come! She ran in the bathroom and I placed the towel underneath me to catch the blood flow as it continued to pour out. I was so scared and I had no idea what was going on. I went and sat on the toilet in hopes that it would stop and it did within a few minutes but those few minutes felt like eternity. I got up to clean myself up and when I turned around to look in the toilet it hit me what had just happened A MISCARRIAGE!! I went into complete shock and began to cry profusely! I couldn't believe what had just happened. My Mom had already contacted the Dr. and they told her to bring me into the ER to have a D and C (Dialation and Curation) a procedure to clean out the remains of the baby from my uterus. I was still in a lot of pain and still sobbing. I remember asking God "Why".

The procedure was very painful and I was only mildly sedated. I can remember laying on the table thinking why did this happen to me. I was getting use to the idea of becoming a mother, however, God had different plans. The next several months were very depressing for me. I couldn't eat or sleep and I pretty much stayed in the house and closed myself off from everyone.

My mom and I were not getting along and she was always on my back about finding a job so that I could move out. One of my closest friend's lived across the street from me and I hung out at her house almost daily. I would always tell my friend about how much my Mom and I argued and how she was always on my back about everything. My girlfriend ended up inviting me to come stay at her house with her and her Mom. This would only be temporary until I could find a job and a place to stay.

My girlfriend and I slept all day and partied all night. This become my regular lifestyle and I felt so much freedom. I didn't have anyone telling me what to do at every moment and it felt great. I was thinking to myself, "why can't my Mom be as laid back as my friend's Mom?" My friend's Mom was a very sweet lady and she treated me just like her own. She gave me a place to stay, she fed me and she supported me. I stayed with my friend for about a year then I moved out and relocated to Durham, N.C. which is where I grew up. It felt good being back around my closest friend. I moved in with one of my best friends and a new chapter began!

Chapter Two Discussion

What are some things that stood out to you in this chapter?

Would you have handled things differently, if so how?

What lessons did you learn if any?

CHAPTER THREE

DOUBLE TROUBLE!

Living with my girlfriend was fun but it was also becoming a little too close for comfort. She only had a one-bedroom apartment and it wasn't built for 2 people. I was grateful that she allowed me to come and stay with her because I had no idea where I would have gone. My girlfriend was a party animal and she seemed to always have a boyfriend that would come visit. I started dating as well, I met this really tall, handsome guy at the grocery store one day. We started spending a lot of time together and of course things became physical very quickly. He wasn't the "typical" type that I normally go for, but I have to admit the sex was AMAZING! (sorry not sorry) Our relationship was like a roller coaster and we couldn't seem to make things work so it ended very quickly for many reasons.

About 3 months later, I started feeling very sick literally every day. I decided to go to the Dr. to get checked out. They ran a few tests and told me that they would call me soon with the results. A week or so passed and received a phone call from my Dr. office. The nurse on the other end said, "we figured out what's wrong with you, you are pregnant with TWINS!" I held the phone in complete shock and my entire body went numb from head to toe. If I hadn't already been sitting down, I think I would have passed out because I felt the blood rush from my head. I hung up the phone and told my girlfriend what the nurse had just told me. She was just as shocked as I was.

I'm now pregnant with twins and I'm trying to wrap my head around this news because it shook my entire world. Now I had to call "him" to tell him that he's about to be a father to not 1 but 2 babies and I knew the conversation wouldn't go well because we were already broken up and had moved on with our lives. When I called to let him know that I was pregnant, of course there was denial on his end that he was the father. He actual told me that he wanted a blood test and I agreed. Now that I'm pregnant with 2 babies I knew that I needed to find somewhere else to live, I think I had gotten on my girlfriend's last nerve at that point.

My next move was to my best friend's house to live with her husband and kid's. Talk about crowded, this was a two-bedroom apartment with 5 of us living there and 2 more babies on the way in a few months. My best friend is an amazing woman, she took me in and cared for me as if I was one of her children. My pregnancy was rough on me and I endured a lot of complications. My pregnancy was considered high risk because I was having twins. I started having Braxton Hicks contractions very early on and I wasn't able to do much of anything but rest.

On September 19, 1991, I gave birth to a son and daughter. They were the most precious things I had ever laid my eyes on. I was now the mother of 2 little ones and I knew my life would be changed forever! How in the world am I supposed to take care of two babies at the same time. I lost my job and didn't have any income coming in. I had to apply for assistance with Social Services to support my children because their father was not around. Adding two more lives to an already cramped living situation was unbearable. As soon as I was able to get one baby asleep the other would awake screaming. It was a constant of cleaning bottles, changing diapers, bathes, feeding, burping, washing clothes and more feedings. Everywhere that I went I had to take two car seats, multiple bottles, a ton of diapers and wipes and a double stroller. Life was so overwhelming and I was mentally and physically exhausted due to the lack of sleep and little help with the babies. My girlfriend helped when she could but she had to take care of her own kids.

After a few short months I ended up moving back home with my Dad and Stepmom. Thank God for the help from my Stepmom, she was so helpful in caring for the babies. Life was truly a struggle and I had no idea which direction to go as far as finding work, child care, and all of the important things it takes to raise kids. My Stepmom and I tagged team with the babies, she would take one and I would have one. This was very helpful and we did the best we could.

Although my Stepmom's help was so beneficial I found that I needed to move back to N.C. to start all over again. Durham here I come back again!

Chapter Three Discussion

What are some things that stood out to you in this chapter?

Would you have handled things differently, if so how?

What lessons did you learn if any?

CHAPTER FOUR

3's A CROWD

The wedding planning was coming along and it was so much fun. I picked out my wedding party, five of my closet friends and the guest list has grown to 125 at this point. I found someone to make my bridemaid's dresses, we have the venue and a caterer. Life is definitely feeling normal and I feel like I have so much to look forward to.

It was time for me to go dress shopping, I was so excited. I didn't have much money to spend but I wanted something simple yet elegant, something memorable. I wanted to see tears in his eyes when I walked down the aisle. This is the moment that all little girl's dream of. My first wedding only lasted two weeks and we didn't have a ceremony, so this wedding meant everything to me and everything had to be perfect.

After weeks and weeks of planning, it's now 2 days before the big event. I'm sitting home finalizing everything and the phone rings. When I answered the phone, the woman on the other end proceeds to ask me a question, she said "Ask him how he plan to marry you while he's still married to me?" I was like "EXCUSE ME, WHO ARE YOU?" She said, "This is his wife!" I said, "what do you mean his wife, he told me that he wasn't with anyone and that he wasn't married." I finally hung up the phone because I couldn't believe what just happened. I waited for him to come home before confronting him.

Tic-toc, tic-toc, I'm watching the clock, second by second waiting for the door to open. Finally, he walked in and he was trying to figure out why I was up so late. I immediately lost it and asked him point blank, "ARE YOU MARRIED?" He didn't hesitate and he looked down and said, "yes." I begin to give him the 3rd degree with my questioning because I didn't understand why he didn't tell me this. We've been planning a wedding all this time and you left out this very important detail.

The explanation that was given to me was that the divorce should have gone through by now and that there were some complications with the paperwork and the divorce can't be granted within the 2 days before my wedding. I got on the phone and immediately started calling my guests, all 125 of them and told them the wedding was called off. I had never felt so humiliated in my life. Of course, everyone was asking what happened, what's wrong, are you ok, yeah all those hard questions that I didn't want to answer. He didn't offer to help make any of the calls and he basically left the house and I never saw him after that. Just like that my life was once again in a shamble and once again that ugly, dark, thing called depression reared it's head again!

Just when I thought things couldn't get any worse, I just returned from a Dr.'s appointment and found out that I'm about 4 weeks pregnant. I immediately called Planned Parenthood and made an appointment to terminate the pregnancy. I'm already raising twins, there's no way possible I can bring another child in this world under these circumstances. The man that I was supposed to marry is gone, I'm all alone with my children and no plans on what to do next. How in the world did I get here, I can't believe that I'm about to terminate this pregnancy, who does that? Father God help me!

Chapter Four Discussion

What are some things that stood out to you in this chapter?

Would you have handled things differently, if so how?

What lessons did you learn if any?

CHAPTER FIVE

THERE'S NO PLACE LIKE HOME

Between the wedding not happening and the constant vertigo, I found myself moving back home to Virginia. I moved back with my Dad and Stepmom until I could figure out what's next. The kids are now almost 3 yrs old and they are getting into everything. My stepmom found out she's pregnant and it was great news for us all. She's been trying to have a baby for years now. She's had 3 miscarriages, of which all were multiple births, so she's finally going to get her bundle of joy. I stayed at the house for about a year, then decided to find a place for me and the kids. It's time that I finally stop running back and forth from house to house and find my own home, lord knows the kids need some stability in their lives.

I applied for public housing and it didn't take long for them to find me a place. I had an okay job but it wasn't paying much. I ended up moving to a housing project which wasn't located in the best part of town, but it was mine and I could finally have something for me and the kids. I got them enrolled in pre-school and we began our new lives in our own place.

I didn't like where we lived, there's a lot of violence in the neighborhood and all I hear day in and out is gunshots. I couldn't let the kids go out and play much because I was afraid for them. I thought that finding my own place would put me in a better space, but I feel trapped in this house because of the fear of getting hurt. The kids started school and I worked every day. Life just trotted along for us, we had a roof over our head, we had food and the kids had what they needed.

I tried to have a social life but it was difficult with the kids around all the time. I didn't have any relief or time to myself, they were always with me. I had friends that would come over and visit from time to time which was nice. I started thinking very heavily about my life and how I needed to really buckle down and figure out this thing called life. I never thought that I would be living in low income housing, I know it's helpful for a lot of people but this is not the plan or goal that I had for myself. I really feel like I'm failing at being a mother to my kids, I know they deserve so much better than what I'm providing. I feel like I'm letting myself down, I've created such a mess of my life and I don't know how I got here and most importantly, I don't know how to fix it.

I woke up today and it really hit me hard that I needed to make a change and fast. I decided to sell what I could and I packed up and moved to Maryland to stay with my girlfriend. I know this was a rash decision, I had no job, no money, other than from the furniture that I sold and no plan what I was going to do in Maryland. Once we got settled in with my girlfriend, I was able to find a job at the mall. It didn't pay much but it allowed me to help my girlfriend with her expenses. It felt good to be in a different city, a city with so much going on. It was a little intimidating because I'd never lived in a large city before. I was able to purchase a vehicle to get me to and from. Still dealing with my head spinning daily it was hard to drive on most days. I ended up missing a couple of payments on the car and it got repossessed. I was blessed that my girlfriend's grandfather offered to take me to work. Things started getting stressful at home, and you can tell that things were different between my girlfriend and I. She opened her home, a 2-bedroom apartment to me and 2 kids, along with her teenage daughter so it was to be expected. Things were crowded and no one really had much privacy but we all did the best that we can. I really appreciated her taking us in. After a few months had passed, my girlfriend decided that she wanted to buy a house. She let me know of her plans, but this meant I had to find somewhere else to live and I wasn't ready or prepared for that at the time. The city where I lived was very expensive and I wasn't making a lot of money so I wasn't sure how I would make this happen. Let the search begin!

Chapter Five Discussion

What are some things that stood out to you in this chapter?

Would you have handled things differently, if so how?

What lessons did you learn if any?

CHAPTER SIX

SOMETHING'S NEVER CHANGE!

I'm having regrets of moving back to Durham, yet again. For some reason I keep finding myself back here with hopes that things will somehow change. I moved back in with my girlfriend. Of course, the living arrangements were minimal, adding me and two small children. I don't like living with people but somehow I've got to figure this thing out.

I was able to find a decent job and eventually found a one- bedroom apartment for me and the twins. It was extremely small and we all shared the one bedroom but more importantly, I finally had my own place. My daycare expenses were killing me, paying for two children that are under 5 years of age is very expensive. Things were a financial strain but I made it work.

One day I was getting ready for work and the entire room started spinning to the point that I had to hold on to the walls to walk. I was scared to death because I had never experienced anything like this. I went to the Dr. a few days later because this spinning feeling wouldn't go away, as a matter of fact it got worse. My initial visit to the Doctor didn't determine anything and I was referred to several specialists to have some test ran. Test after test after test and still no answers. After about 6 months of running back and forth to the doctor, I was finally told that I have something called vertigo. I had no idea what that meant and I'd never heard of it before. I was basically told that I'm dizzy for no reason and that I would more than likely have to deal with this the rest of my life! To say that I was shocked would be an understatement. What do you mean, I would have to deal with this the rest of my life?"

My world continued to spin day and night, the spinning would not stop. I was put on several medications to try to control the dizziness but nothing worked. I was raising two small children, trying to function as normal as possible with my head spinning from the time I woke up, until the time I went to bed. The spinning got so bad that I could no longer drive my car. I ended up losing my job because I was calling out sick so much. Things got worse and worse and that ugly demon called depression reared it's ugly head in the worst way! Lord WHY ME, WHY?

My day to day life was unbearable and I have no idea how I was making it day in and out, well let me rephrase that, it's nothing but God's grace and mercy that's getting me through. In the midst of all the chaos I started to talking to this guy that I met through a friend of mine. It was a pleasant distraction, considering everything that I had going. Things moved pretty quickly with us and we began to get serious. After a few months of dating he moved in with me and helped me with my bills and the kids. He was a great provider and he loved my kids to death. He took me to meet his family in South Carolina and they were happy that we found each other. Shortly after we returned back from that visit, I received a proposal of marriage. Of course I accepted, I was feeling blessed that this man came into the picture and treated my kids as his own and more importantly he loved me and showed me that he loved me. Yes, let's get married!

I immediately started planning the wedding, I didn't want to have a long engagement. Things started to feel normal again even though my head was still spinning all the time, but at least I had someone by my side and I was no longer alone. Something good finally happened and it felt amazing! Guess what y'all I'm getting married!

Chapter Six Discussion

What are some things that stood out to you in this chapter?

Would you have handled things differently, if so how?

What lessons did you learn if any?

CHAPTER SEVEN

CRAZY IS AS CRAZY DOES

I was able to find a really nice 2- bedroom apartment not far from where I was and it was close to my job. I also found a better paying job through a temp service. The apartment was very expensive but I had to figure out how to make this work. My girlfriend gave me some of her furniture and I purchased a few items, so I had the bare minimum. It felt good to be in my own space and the kids now had their own room where they could play. I enrolled the kids in the elementary school that was close by. Things seemed to be falling into place, slowly but surely.

I had recently spoken with a friend who was telling me about this telephone dating service. I decided that I was ready to be involved in a serious relationship, now that I had my own place. I spoke to several different men and found the process to be very exhausting to say the least. I stumbled across this guy named Tony, he seemed to be someone that I could get serious with. What I respected the most about him is the fact that he was raising his 3 year old son and had full custody of him. We had great conversation and we has a lot in common. Tony and I got serious pretty quickly, to the point that I allowed him to move in with me and the kids. I knew in my heart of hearts that this wasn't a good idea but I needed help with the bills and his lease was up at his place so we went with it.

Right away I started noticing that Tony like to smoke week and drink a lot. He would go to several happy hour spots after work almost daily. He would come home high and drunk which meant he would more than likely start an argument with me. Things started to get very uncomfortable, I hated arguing with him especially around the kids. Tony, walked in the door from a nigh out at the bar with his co-workers, I went downstairs to check on the laundry. When I got back I attempted to open the front door but it was locked. Tony was on the other side yelling at me and laughing that he wasn't going to open the door. He thought it was funny and took it as a joke. I didn't find it funny at all, it was cold outside and I didn't have a coat. After about 30 minutes he finally opened the door and let me in. At this point I'm extremely upset and we immediately began arguing. He was on one side of the room and I was on the other. I looked away for a moment and when I turned around I saw the recliner chair from the living room coming toward me. This fool picked up the chair and threw it at me! I was completely dumbfounded, nervous and scared all at the same time. Tony just showed me how serious his angered could get really get. I ducked and ran upstairs, in that moment all I could think about is "what have I gotten myself into."

Things were really stressful around the house, the tension was very thick. Tony and I basically walked by each other not speaking. We went to work came home and went to separate rooms. He still wanted to argue every day but I would ignore him. I swear, I really know how to pick them.

Chapter Seven Discussion

What are some things that stood out to you in this chapter?

Would you have handled things differently, if so how?

What lessons did you learn if any?

CHAPTER EIGHT

BREAK UP TO NEVER MAKE UP!

Things were still very rocky with Tony and I and they were only getting worse. I decided it was time to break things off because he was too violent, he drank to much and he basically had no respect for me and my kids. More importantly, as a mother, it was my job to protect my children and provide them a safe environment. It's Sunday afternoon and Tony was on his keyboard practicing a song that he wrote. He enjoyed writing music and aspired to be a singer one day. This was another thing that I loved about him, but all of the negativity that he brought to the relationship outweighed anything positive that he did.

I decided that now was a better time than never to let him know that I no longer wanted to be in a relationship with him. I was standing on the stairs as I was having the conversation with him.

He didn't say much and continued playing the keyboard. Within seconds as I proceed to walk up the stairs, he jumped up from his chair and came running behind me and threw me over his shoulder and ran up the stairs with me barely hanging on. I had no clue what was about to happen but I knew it wasn't good. He slammed me into the wall and began to curse at me. All could do is try to fight my way loose but his strength was too much for me. The kids stood in the doorway of their room watching this all take place. Tony threw me over his shoulder again, this time taking me into our bedroom. He body slammed me to the floor, diving on top of me. One of my arms was behind my back when I feel to the floor and it felt like it was broker. Within what seemed to be hours but was only a few seconds he attempted to pick me up off of the floor trying to throw me out of our bedroom window. I was able to stop him, and it was really strange because in that moment this monster suddenly turned into warm, calming person who was now worried about how bad he hurt me. He tried to console me and kept asking me if I was okay. I told him to get a way from me as I screamed in shear terror. I couldn't process what had just happened and I was in complete shock. I got up from the floor and I couldn't feel my arm, it was numb. I walked downstairs to the kitchen and grabbed a knife out of the drawer. The only thing on my mind right now is, killing this man! The kids were screaming and as I proceeded up the stairs with the knife, I couldn't go through with it because the kids were watching me.

Tony knew that he had messed up so he left the house. I didn't know what to do in this moment. Call the police? Call my friend? Call my Mom? I'm hysterical, I'm in pain and I'm not thinking clearly. I went to calm the kids down and then I called my Mom to tell her what happened. My Mother was an emotionless person, she really didn't show much empathy so I'm not sure why I called her but I did. I began screaming and crying trying to explain to her what happened. Of course her comment was, "you shouldn't have let a stranger move in with you!" That really hurt because this wasn't the time for her to say that to me. Her next comment to me was, "what would you like for me to do, I'm all the way in North Carolina?"

I immediately hung up on her, I couldn't take how she was treating me after what I had just went through. I found myself scared and alone with no one to turn too. I decided not to contact the police because I was afraid of what he would do next. I knew that if I called the police he could possibly lose custody of his son. Tony came back a few days later, he tried to apologize but I didn't want to hear it. I told him to get his things and GET OUT!! He begged me to allow him to stay for 30 days. He had just started a new job and he would get his first two paychecks within that 30 days. Against my better judgement I agreed to it. I was still afraid of what he would do next. The agreement was he would stay upstairs out of my way I would stay downstairs. My thinking was I could at least hear him walking if he decided to come downstairs at some point to finish what he started. Waiting for those 30 days felt like a lifetime.

Tony kept his word and moved out in exactly 30 days later. I'm now left to figure out how to get my life back together. I'm so broken, vulnerable and now I get to call myself something that I swore I would never call myself, a domestic abuse survivor! I never sought help, I never talked about what happened and pretty much buried this deep within. I'm at a point where I'm really starting to wonder why I'm still here. My best friend, depression, once again shows up and takes over. I think the dark hole is permanently becoming my residence.

Chapter Eight Discussion

What are some things that stood out to you in this chapter?

Would you have handled things differently, if so how?

What lessons did you learn if any?

CHAPTER NINE

PEACING THE PIECES BACK TOGETHER

Things are still very foggy and confusing even though Tony left a couple of months ago. I'm still pushing through the depression and vertigo. It's crazy that you have to walk around with your head spinning 24 hours a day and there's not one doctor to tell you why. The twins are now attending their new school and I'm trying to keep things as normal as possible around the house. My bills are really starting to pile up on me, I got use to Tony helping with some of the expenses. Having to pay for a taxi everyday to get back and forth to work has gotten to be very expensive. Every since I was diagnosed with vertigo, I haven't been able to drive much. The motion of the car makes the vertigo worse and it's difficult to find you balance while driving.

I met a taxi driver who started to pick me up on regular basis. He's a really nice guy and very pleasant. Every morning when he picks me up for work he greets me with a smile. He's very laid back and very kind. I told him about the recent abuse that I went through and he was so empathetic and caring. He even started giving me free rides to work, which I greatly appreciated. He would also pick up the kids from school for me and he mad sure they didn't need anything. As our friendship started to progress, we kind of started to date. I say kind of because I liked him but I was afraid of dating or having another relationship. The taxi driver is from another country, we had a few things in common but not many. I think I was simply drawn to his kindness, especially coming out of an abusive relationship, I didn't know how to receive kindness any longer.

The taxi driver and I now together for some months, decided to move in together. Even though I was in such a vulnerable state, the only thing that I could think of was, not having to pay bills by myself anymore. We decided that I would move in with him because he had more room than I had at my apartment. His townhome was really nice a very spacious. He lived in a really nice neighborhood and the kids loved their new environment. The kids also loved him, he became a father figure in their life. He was consistent and always there for us. After I got settled in the new house, we began discussing marriage. There wasn't a proposal but for me I felt that if we were going to be living together we should be married.

I began planning this huge wedding. This man made sure that I had everything that I needed. He didn't want to work and he took care of all the bills. I started to see that this is how a real man should treat a woman. My feelings started to grow day by day and I started to feel very blessed to find him. I felt very safe with him and not once did I question if he would cheat on me or abuse me. He made my world feel okay again.

The wedding is fast approaching and I had everything ready and organized. I started attending cosmetology school since I wasn't working. I've always wanted to be a beautician and I was excited about this opportunity. I was excited knowing that all of my friends and family would be attending my wedding. I rented a small recreation facility to have the wedding and the reception.

I've always dreamed of wearing a beautiful wedding gown with a long train and veil. It's my wedding day and my nerves are all over the place. There's an unnerving feeling in my stomach and something is telling me that I shouldn't do this. I guess all of the things that I've been through are starting to hit me. I feel like nothing good is suppose to happen for me at this point.

It's almost time for me to walk down the isle and as I'm looking around I realized that my father never showed up. I'm so angry because once again, he's not there for me. I asked my step father would he mind walking me down the aisle. I couldn't believe my father didn't show and he didn't have the decency to call and tell me that he couldn't attend. I often wonder, what have I done to this man for him to keep disappointing me.

The wedding was beautiful and I loved having all of my friends and family there. I'm officially married and for some reason I still have this feeling in my stomach that doesn't feel to good.

Life is pretty good for the most part. I'm noticing some little things about my husband that I'd never noticed before. A lot of things were simply due to our different cultural backgrounds. I was content for the most part, I didn't need or want for anything but I couldn't shake that feeling in the pit of my stomach. As time went on I finally started to realize that I married a man that I wasn't in love with. I realized that I settled for this marriage because this man came into my life at one of the worse moments of my life and he made it all better. I loved him as a person and I loved the fact that he loved me and my kids.

We started arguing a lot because I was withholding sex on a regular basis, I wasn't interested in my wifely duties and he had a problem with it and he let me know it. I tried to change my mindset but it wasn't working. All of sudden it hit me, I'm not happy and I want out. It's now 364 days into the marriage and I packed me and the kids up and left. I bet you a million dollars you will never guess whoro I moved to, yes Durham, NC.

Chapter Nine Discussion

What are some things that stood out to you in this chapter?

Would you have handled things differently, if so how?

What lessons did you learn if any?

CHAPTER TEN

HOPING THE SUNSHINE STATE IS SUNNY

Once again I'm on the move Durham wasn't it for me, I felt stuck and just couldn't seem to get things together. My sister, cousin convinced me to start fresh by moving to Florida. I was very hesitant because it's so far away from everyone but I figured why not nothing else has worked up to this point. I was able to land a job and a very nice apartment before I moved to Florida. I actually started getting very excited about the transition. I was able to get packed up in a week and my cousin came to get me and the kids. We spent about 12 hours on the road but we finally made it there. Florida is absolutely beautiful and it's definitely a different environment. The kids and I got settled in pretty quickly. My job was with a major credit card company and it was great meeting new people. What's interesting about moving here, I started seeing my cousin less and less. I thought moving here would bring us closer together but that's not the case. It felt like I was living in this new place all alone but I adapted.

The weather here is extremely hot and humid but the palm trees and the atmosphere is amazing. I think I could live here forever. I was able to take the kids to Disney, which is something I've dreamed of. The parks are huge and there's a lot of walking involved but the kids and I had a blast. We also visited Daytona Beach which wasn't far from where we lived. It feels like things are finally starting to look up for a change. The kids met a lot of kids and we lived in a really nice neighborhood.

My job is very interesting it's a call center and it's a very busy place. I've met some cool people that I eat lunch with every day. Florida seems to be a good move and I'm excited to see what's in store. One morning when I got to work, I had to go use the restroom. I noticed some blood on the tissue and immediately got alarmed. I went back to my desk to make a doctor's appointment. For the next several days my mind was going crazy trying to figure out why that blood was there. It was finally appointment day, my doctor had scheduled me to have a CT scan to see what they're able to find.

The procedure wasn't too bad, I had to have some dye injected into my veins so that the doctor could have a clearer picture. I received a call a couple of days after the scan and what I heard on the other end rendered me speechless. The doctor told me that the scan showed a "spot" on my liver. They couldn't determine if it was cancerous or not but they wanted to schedule a biopsy immediately. By the time I heard the words cancer, my body went totally numb. I called my Mom and other family members to let them know what was determined. Immediately my Mom and stepmom told me that I needed to move back home. They felt like Florida was too far away from them and they wouldn't be able to come down to help me with the kids during my biopsy.

As I'm listening to them trying to convince me from moving back to VA, my conscious was screaming at me not to do it. I never liked living in VA and I always felt stuck and unaccomplished there. I continued to process what was said and decided it would be best if I moved home. If it turned out to be cancer I would definitely need help with the kids, so we packed it and back on the road we.

One of my closest childhood friends came to Florida to pick me and up and we drove a Uhaul back to VA. I made an appointment with local Dr. to determine next steps. Another scan was set up, however, the results this time were different. No "spots" were found and the Dr. told me that there was no need for a biopsy. Puzzled and confused at this point, all I could think is, what the heck is really going.

It was a relief knowing that nothing was found, but I'm not happy that I left my newfound life in Florida. Apparently, there's a reason I needed to move back to VA., I not sure why but I'm a firm believer that everything happens for a reason. Let's see what's in store, I swear this feels like Groundhog Day!

Chapter Ten Discussion

What are some things that stood out to you in this chapter?

Would you have handled things differently, if so how?

What lessons did you learn if any?

THINGS TO REMEMBER WHEN TRYING TO MOVE FORWARD

1. It's normal to not always make the best choices-learn from your mistakes

2. Seek help after going through a tragedy

3. Find someone you can confide in, everyone is not out to hurt you

4. Take accountability for your actions

5. Don't blame others for your choices

6. Write down your thoughts and feelings (journal)

7. FORGIVE YOURSELF, YOU'RE HUMAN

ABOUT THE AUTHOR

LaVonne Gravely Sanders, is a devoted mother, grandmother, sister and friend. LaVonne is also the Founder and CEO of Whew We, LLC, a Women's Empowerment group started to bridge the gap of women supporting and networking with one another. LaVonne created Whew We as a platform where women can discuss the hard topics that we tend to ignore. LaVonne has hosted multiple conferences, created a talk show and several podcasts. She believes that women are powerful individuals but if we came together, we could accomplish so much more.

Email: lavonne_gravely@yahoo.com

Website: https://linktr.ee/whewwe

www.ingramcontent.com/pod-product-compliance
Lightning Source LLC
LaVergne TN
LVHW051200080426

835508LV00021B/2728